Yellow Umbrella Books are published by Capstone Press
151 Good Counsel Drive, P.O. Box 669, Mankato, Minnesota 56002
www.capstonepress.com

Library of Congress Cataloging-in-Publication Data
Reed, Janet (Janet C.)
    Parts of a whole / by Janet Reed.
    p. cm.
    Summary: Simple text and photographs introduce the concept of fractions and
how they can be used to share treats fairly.
    ISBN 0-7368-2935-0 (hardcover)—ISBN 0-7368-2894-X (softcover)
    1. Fractions—Juvenile literature. [1. Fractions. 2. Sharing.] I. Title.
QA117.R44 2004
513.2'6—dc21   2003010969

Editorial Credits
Editorial Director: Mary Lindeen
Editor: Jennifer VanVoorst
Photo Researcher: Wanda Winch
Developer: Raindrop Publishing

Photo Credits
Cover: Erin Hogan/Photodisc; Title Page: C Squared Studios/Photodisc; Page 2–Page
6: Gary Sundermeyer/Capstone Press; Page 7: Comstock; Page 8–Page 16: Gary
Sundermeyer/Capstone Press; Page 2 (background): Andy Sotiriou/Photodisc; Page
5–Page 6 (background): Nancy R. Cohen/Photodisc; Page 8 (background): Ryan
McVay/Photodisc; Page 9 (background): David Buffington/Photodisc; Page 10
(background): Ryan McVay/Photodisc; Page 12 (background): Buccina Studios/
Photodisc; Page 15–Page 16 (background): Nancy R. Cohen/Photodisc

Parts of a Whole

by Janet Reed

Consultants: David Olson, Director of Undergraduate Studies, and Tamara Olson, PhD, Associate Professor, Department of Mathematical Sciences, Michigan Technological University

Yellow Umbrella Books

an imprint of Capstone Press
Mankato, Minnesota

Wholes

You can eat an apple.
You can eat the whole thing.

You can also eat the apple in parts. When you eat a whole apple, you eat all the parts.

You can eat a whole orange.
These parts make up a whole
orange.

When you eat a whole orange,
you eat all the parts.

Halves

You can eat a whole sandwich.
You can also eat it in parts.
This sandwich is in two parts.

The two parts are the same size. Each part is called one half. Two halves make up a whole sandwich.

Two halves always make a
whole. Half of this glass is
filled with milk. Half of this
glass is empty.

Does this girl have a half or a whole glass of juice?

Thirds

Here is a whole pie. How can these three friends share the pie?

They can divide the pie into three equal parts. Each of these equal parts is called one third. Three thirds make up a whole.

Fourths

How can these four friends share a pear? They can divide the pear into four equal parts.

Each of these equal parts is called one fourth. Four fourths make up a whole.

This fruit has been divided into parts. Is it divided into halves or thirds? Is it divided into fourths?

Here's one whole pizza.
Each child wants a slice.
Should the pizza be divided
into halves, thirds, or fourths?

Parts of a Whole

Halves, thirds, and fourths
are all parts of a whole.
You can split things into
many parts when you share!

Words to Know/Index

Word Count: 252
Early-Intervention Level: 15